21 LIFE LESSONS FOR TEENAGE BOYS

Most Important Life Lessons I wish I knew When I was a Teen

Ali Welch

This book is published by Smart Teens Publishers

ISBN: **979-8-9886895-9-1**

Paperback Edition

First Edition: 2023

Table of Contents

Table of Contents

Introduction

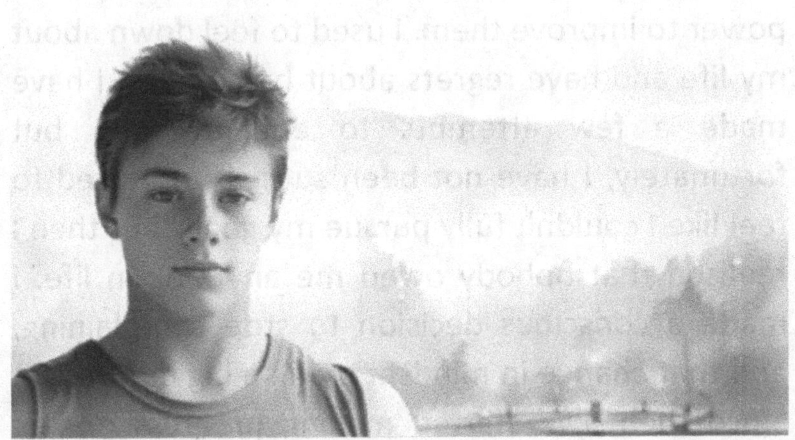

When I was growing up, I didn't have a father or mentor to guide me on the path to success. I had to learn the ropes through trial and error, facing numerous challenges, and finding my way. That's why I want to share with you 21 lessons that I wish someone had told me when I was your age. I hope that by sharing these lessons, you can avoid some of the difficulties I faced and have a better start in life.

You should realize that nobody is going to rescue you, including your parents, teachers, and even your closest friends. To achieve true success in life, it is important to develop the ability to rely on oneself. This means that you need to fully acknowledge and embrace your current circumstances, even if they are difficult, and recognize that you are the only person who has the power to improve them. I used to feel down about my life and have regrets about being born. I have made a few attempts to end my life, but fortunately, I have not been successful. I used to feel like I couldn't fully pursue my goals, but then I realized that nobody owed me anything in life. I made a conscious decision to stop complaining, and that change in mindset made a big difference. Since then, I've started making progress on my journey.

To build up your confidence, it's important to be mindful of the words you use. Our daily thoughts and speech shape the person we will become in the future. You know, I've noticed that when I spend time with really successful people, they never complain or speak negatively about themselves or others. It's interesting because when I was a teenager, I used to do both of those things all the time, and I didn't realize the impact it had. When I was younger, I used to harm myself and my confidence. But everything changed when I turned 16. My teacher gave me a challenge: to go an entire month without complaining and see how it would positively impact my life. It was a difficult challenge, but it continues to be my guiding principle even now. As time went on, I realized how frequently I engaged in this behavior. I decided to alter my speaking style and actively avoid complaining, even in situations as minor as waiting in line. Instead of expressing my lack of skill in this area, I would focus on identifying areas for improvement and finding ways to enhance my abilities.

Guess what? At the end of that month, a small change happened that completely shifted the course of my life. It was shortly after that I realized my strong love for cooking, started exploring it, and earned my first dollar from it.

I would like to share the mistakes I made and the actions I took that have led me to where I am today. I rarely complain or speak negatively about myself, and I encourage you to do the same for the next 30 days. Pay attention to how your life changes, as every word and action has consequences. Even seemingly insignificant actions can have a significant impact over time, whether positive or negative. It's important to live with intention and take responsibility for your actions. Spending hours on TikTok or playing video games may seem harmless, but they can gradually affect your dopamine levels and ability to focus on important things. On the other hand, reading for just 10 minutes a day may seem boring, but over time, it can accumulate knowledge, improve your focus, and make you a better person.

Just remember that God is aware of everything you do. It's important to live your life as if someone is always observing your actions. The small choices you make today have an impact on the person you become in the future. Looking back, one regret I have from my teenage years is starting to smoke marijuana. I strongly advise against doing it because it has been one of the worst decisions I have ever made. I suggest that you avoid it completely, especially while you are still young.

I had never tried alcohol or drugs for 16 years, but during my last year of high school, I gave in to peer pressure and decided to smoke a joint for the first time. I enjoyed it so much that it became something I couldn't get enough of. For the next eight years of my life, I did something almost every single day, with breaks in between. Did it completely ruin everything? I'm not sure about that. Even though I managed to maintain my physical well-being, have a social circle, and even establish my cooking business, I developed a reliance on smoking to find pleasure in every aspect of my life. For years, I didn't have much interest in doing anything unless it involved some level of involvement. This included activities like going to the gym, having lunch, and, of course, going to sleep. Unfortunately, the most challenging aspect is that it caused lasting damage to my brain, which I still struggle with even now.

When you smoke as a teenager, it can have lasting effects on your memory and cognitive ability. This is because, during these formative years, your brain is still in the process of developing. I didn't know about it in the past, and I regret not knowing because it continues to have an impact on me even now. Additionally, it's incredibly addictive. If someone ever told you that it wasn't addictive, they were likely addicted themselves. I only came to this realization after attempting to quit. For four weeks, I felt miserable, unable to sleep, sweating excessively at night, and barely having any appetite. I faced a significant challenge that my body strongly desired, but eventually, I had a breakthrough. I experienced a newfound sense of mental clarity that I had not previously encountered, and it made me feel like my true self once more. I experienced a significant change in my life, which turned out to be one of the most impactful transformations I've ever gone through. As a result, I haven't smoked for more than two years now. Interestingly, this period has been incredibly successful for me. Looking back, I would advise myself to avoid smoking during that time because it's crucial to prioritize the well-being of our minds. After all, our mind is our most powerful tool.

We have to be mindful of the fact that we only have one brain. In today's world, it is increasingly easy to harm our brains due to the abundance of technology and distractions. These elements are specifically created to grab our attention and harm our cognitive abilities. So, it's important to be cautious about the type of content you engage with every day and prioritize activities that positively impact your mental well-being before it becomes a problem. The most impactful action I took to develop a resilient mindset was embracing stoicism. I wanted to share that stoicism has had a profound impact on my life and has been a significant factor in my current success. Being stoic means acknowledging and embracing the world as it is without attempting to alter things that are beyond our control. This is the key that brings me happiness and inner peace. It's important to recognize that each of us has unique circumstances in life. We are not influenced by factors like the country we were born in or the racial background we have, whether we are black or white. You can control how you perceive these things. Do you categorize them as positive or negative? A stoic person observes the world as it truly is, without attaching labels or judgments to anything. I agree with Shakespeare's words: Things aren't inherently good or bad; it's our perception that determines their nature.

The way we perceive and react to the things that happen to us determines their impact on us. Surprisingly, some of the most challenging events in my life turned out to be the most significant blessings in disguise. When I was younger, my family lost our house because we couldn't afford the mortgage payments. As a result, we had to move in with a family friend (Jason), and it was a really difficult and emotional day for me. I started working at a grocery store which I later used part of for a cafeteria. It was during this experience my love for cooking intensified. If that particular event hadn't occurred, I suppose I wouldn't be having this conversation with you right now. If you want to succeed, it's important to embrace a stoic philosophy and be prepared to experience failure. Failure is a necessary step towards achieving great success, so it's important to welcome it and not be afraid to fail more often.

Unfortunately, our school system has taught us over the years to view failure in a negative light. That's unfortunate. If you were to introduce me to any highly successful individual, I can assure you that they have experienced countless failures along the way. This is because trial and error is the only method through which one can truly master anything in life. This is the way things work, and it's important to show respect for how things are done. Hey, I just wanted to let you know that right now is a great moment for you to start this journey. Even if things don't go as planned, it's not as terrible as it may seem. Before I made my first million dollars, I experienced failure with various businesses over seven years.

It is important to always honor the commitments you make, especially when they are promises you have made to yourself. Imagine this scenario: If you were to invite your friends to dinner every week but consistently failed to show up, would you expect them to hold you in high regard? The promises we make to ourselves are just the same. If you consistently set your alarm for 7 a.m. but end up hitting the snooze button until 10 a.m. every day, it can gradually diminish your self-respect. This behavior, when repeated over time, can eventually lead to a significant decrease in your overall self-respect. I assure you, this is a straightforward principle that will have a lasting impact on your life. It is important to always fulfill the promises you make to others and, equally importantly, to yourself. If you truly value yourself, it is important to make your health a top priority.

In my opinion, not taking care of your body by consuming unhealthy food and being inactive is a genuine expression of self-dislike. If you genuinely cared for and valued yourself, you would take good care of your body as if it were a sacred place. In this lifetime, we are given only one chance, and it's important to remember that it is much more delicate than we often realize. Start taking care of your health now instead of waiting until you're older. Begin right away, and the most effective approach is to be in the company of individuals who share your sentiments. When I was in school, I used to meet people like this through sports, specifically basketball, and by playing music. I suggest you consider getting involved in at least one of these activities because they offer significant advantages. Both sports and music teach you valuable skills through practice, help you understand the importance of teamwork in achieving goals, and introduce you to a community of people who share similar interests.

When I was in school, I used to play basketball. Even though I wasn't very good at it, those moments hold a special place in my heart as some of my favorite childhood memories. They also helped shape me into the person I am today. Meeting some of my closest friends happened this way. During my time in high school, I had a wide circle of acquaintances, but I didn't have many close friends. In reality, I only had two close friends, and we all shared the same goal: to succeed in life. Because of this, I was always careful in selecting my friends, and I believe you should do the same.

I've learned a really important lesson: having a single, reliable friend who shares your core values is much more valuable than being popular and having a large group of friends. If you want to achieve speed, it's better to go by yourself. However, if you want to achieve long-lasting success, it's important to work together with the right people. Your true friends and, above all, your family are the ones who will always be there for you. That's why it's crucial to express gratitude to your parents before it's too late.

Hey, I want to talk to you about something important. If you're fortunate to have your parents around, it's really important to show them love and respect. They brought you into this world, which is an incredible gift. And if you're a teenager listening to this, chances are your parents have provided you with a phone, a home, and internet access. Sometimes we can take these things for granted, but it's important to appreciate them. It doesn't matter what happened to you when you were young; you need to grow into a resilient individual who can forgive and demonstrate love to them while they are still present in your life. Always remember the sacrifices your parents made to raise you, and never forget their efforts. I regret that I took too much time to forgive my father and express my respect and gratitude towards him. I held onto my feelings of anger and resentment towards him for not being there for me when I was younger until I reached the age of 22. It was at that point that I decided to let go of those negative emotions. Unfortunately, just as we were starting to develop a relationship, he passed away from cancer. I still feel a deep sense of regret about this, even to this day.

Make sure to express your love to your parents every day without delay, and most importantly, cherish the experience of being a child in the present moment. You are considered one of the richest individuals in the world because you possess the invaluable asset of youth, which is often regarded as the most valuable form of wealth. Some billionaires are willing to switch lives with you, and time will pass quickly, leaving you wondering where it all went. As you grow older, life will change and become less carefree than it is now. So, occasionally, stay up until 4 a.m., spend the whole night playing games with your friends, laugh for hours about the girls you've met, and find joy in silly things. Embrace your freedom and have fun because, ultimately, these moments will become cherished memories. Make them meaningful and worthwhile.

Hey there, teenagers! Get ready for an in-depth account of my life's ups and downs, how I overcame challenges and achieved success, and how it relates to the 21 important life lessons you should be aware of as a teenager.

Chapter 1: Be comfortable being alone

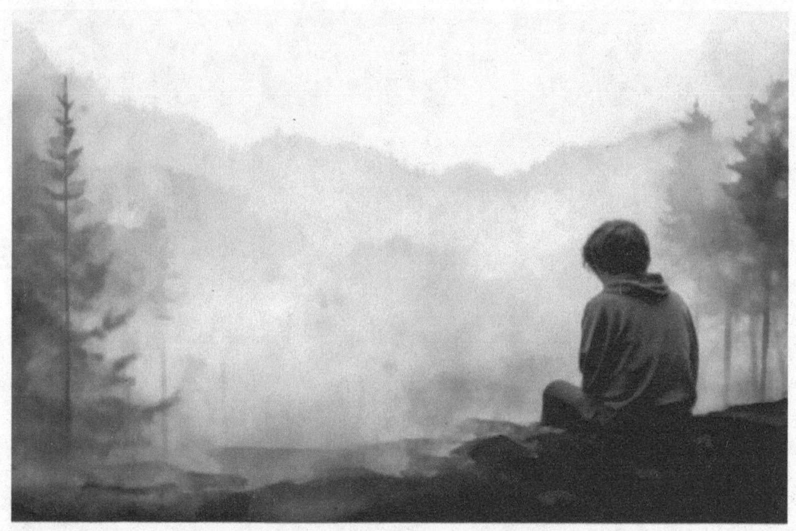

I was thirteen when I first realized the significance of solitude. Growing up without a father was never easy. I constantly felt the gaping void of his absence, like an unfinished puzzle with a missing piece. My peers had fathers teaching them how to ride bikes, tie their first tie, or fix things around the house. I had none of that. No mentor to guide me through the maze of adolescence. But it was during those solitary moments that I stumbled upon the first lesson of my life.

It was a breezy Saturday afternoon, and I was sitting by my bedroom window, watching kids play in the park nearby. Their laughter echoed in the distance, while I fondled aimlessly with a stress toy. A thought hit me: "Maybe I'm destined to be alone." At that moment, it wasn't sadness that washed over me, but a weird sense of relief. I started to explore the beauty of being on my own.

Soon, weekends became my retreats. I visited the local library and spent hours lost in the world of books. These stories taught me more about life than any mentor ever could. Characters became my friends, their challenges resonated with my struggles, and their triumphs became mine. My love for books eventually led me to join a book club, where I met individuals who appreciated my unique perspective. I realized that solitude had sharpened my observation skills, made me more empathetic, and gave me an imagination that most kids my age lacked.

One evening, as I settled into my reading nook, Mrs. Thompson, our elderly neighbor, knocked on our door. She had recently lost her husband and felt lonely. Knowing my penchant for stories, she wondered if I'd read to her occasionally. Those sessions with Mrs. Thompson became more than just reading. We'd share stories, laugh at our jokes, and sometimes sit in comfortable silence, each lost in our thoughts.

From those moments, I realized that being comfortable with my solitude didn't mean I had to be lonely. It meant that I could cherish my own company, reflect, grow, and then step into the world with a renewed sense of purpose.

To all the teenagers out there, it's okay not to be surrounded by people all the time. Embrace those quiet moments. They hold more power than you think. Being comfortable alone is the foundation of self-awareness, understanding, and growth. Because if you can't be at peace with your own company, how can you truly appreciate the company of others?

So, lesson number one? Be comfortable being alone. Because in that solitude, you'll find parts of yourself that you never knew existed.

Chapter 2: Watch your words

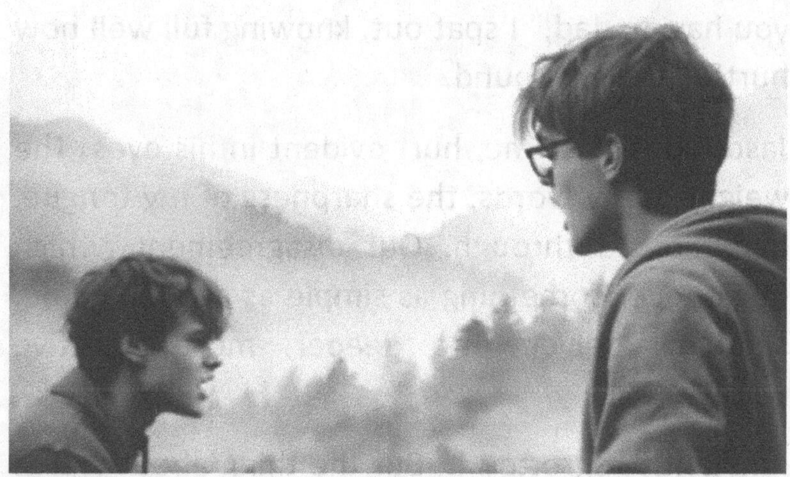

When I was growing up, I had a best friend named Jason. We practically grew up together, two peas in a pod. We had many similarities, but our backgrounds were different. I grew up without a father figure, always trying to understand my place in the world. Jason, on the other hand, had both parents but faced his own set of challenges.

One day, we disagreed over something trivial. You know, the kind of squabbles teenagers often find themselves embroiled in. In the heat of the moment, feeling the need to defend myself and fueled by a concoction of teenage hormones and frustrations from my struggles, I said some words that I would regret for a very long time.

"I bet you think you're better than me just because you have a dad," I spat out, knowing full well how hurtful it might sound.

Jason looked at me, hurt evident in his eyes. The weight of my words, the sharpness of my tongue, had pierced through. Our disagreement, which began over something as simple as a video game, suddenly delved into deeper, more sensitive waters.

I instantly regretted it. But the thing about words is, once they're out there, you can't take them back. It's like trying to put toothpaste back in its tube.

We didn't talk for weeks after that. The guilt ate at me, knowing that my words had created a rift in our friendship. I had always told myself that I wouldn't let my lack of a father or mentor define who I was. Yet, in that moment of vulnerability, I had let it out and used it as a weapon.

One day, after what felt like an eternity, I gathered the courage to apologize. Sitting on the steps of our usual hangout spot, I told Jason how sorry I was. Thankfully, he forgave me, but he also shared how my words had reminded him of the expectations and pressures he felt from his own family.

The lesson I learned that day wasn't just about watching what you say. It was about understanding that everyone has their battles and their insecurities. Just because someone seems to have it all on the surface doesn't mean they aren't dealing with their own set of problems.

That day, I made a promise to myself. To be more thoughtful with my words. To understand that they hold power. Power to hurt, but also power to heal. It's a lesson I'd carry with me throughout my life, and one I hope all teenagers understand early on. Words can build bridges, but they can also burn them. Choose them wisely.

Chapter 3: Every action has a consequence

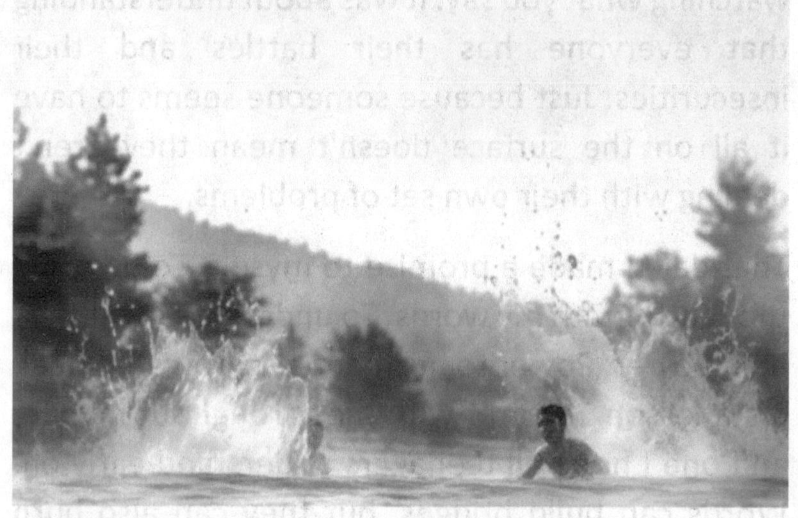

As a teenager, it sometimes felt like the world was against me. With no one to lean on or seek advice from, I made mistakes, but it was from these very mistakes that I learned one of the most valuable life lessons: Every action has a consequence.

It was a warm summer afternoon, and I was 15. The school was out, and the world was my playground. My friend Jason and I had this rebellious spirit that often led us into uncharted territories. One day, on a whim, we decided to sneak into the local swimming pool after hours. The allure of having the entire pool to ourselves, without the scolding of lifeguards or the chatter of other kids, was too much to resist. We climbed the fence and landed, giggling, on the other side.

For a while, it was perfect. The moonlight glimmered on the water, and we felt invincible. But as we were splashing around, we didn't notice the security guard approaching. In our haste to escape, Jason slipped, hurting his ankle. I had a choice to make: leave my friend and save myself or face the consequences of our actions.

I chose to stay with Jason. We were caught, and the consequences were immediate. We were banned from the pool for the entire summer, and our parents were called. Jason's injury wasn't severe, but it meant weeks of discomfort for him and a lasting reminder of our misadventure.

The following weeks were filled with self-reflection. My choices led not only to my suffering but also harmed my friend. The weight of responsibility bore down on me. Every evening, as I looked out of my window, seeing other kids laughing and enjoying their summer, I was reminded of the choices I made and the consequences that followed.

The guilt of causing Jason's injury haunted me. It wasn't just about being caught; it was the realization that my actions had hurt someone I cared about. I visited Jason every day, trying to make amends in any small way I could. It was during these visits that our bond strengthened. We spoke about our dreams, our fears, and our aspirations. Jason shared with me stories of his grandfather, who he looked up to. Through these tales, I realized the importance of guidance and mentorship in one's life.

Determined to not let our mistakes define us, Jason and I started a small community initiative, teaching younger kids the importance of choices and consequences. Every weekend, we gathered a group of kids from the neighborhood, using fun activities and real-life stories to instill life lessons. The process was healing. By acknowledging our mistakes and turning them into lessons for others, we were taking responsibility for our actions and ensuring that others didn't repeat them.

Years went by, and our initiative gained recognition. Schools invited us to share our stories, emphasizing the importance of understanding the consequences of one's actions. It was through this journey that I understood my true calling. I didn't need a father figure to guide me. My mistakes, my experiences, and my desire to make amends became my mentors.

As I stand today, a successful individual, it's not the achievements that I am most proud of; it's the lessons I've learned along the way. My journey, filled with its fair share of pitfalls, has been my greatest teacher. And if there's one lesson I'd want every teenage boy and girl to remember, it's this: Every choice you make will shape your future, so choose wisely. Every action has a consequence, whether immediate or delayed, and it's our responsibility to own up to them and learn.

Life will throw challenges your way. Sometimes you'll have guidance, and sometimes you'll feel utterly alone. But remember, every mistake is a lesson in disguise. Embrace them, learn from them, and grow. Because at the end of the day, it's not about the falls, but how you rise after them.

Chapter 4: Don't smoke weed

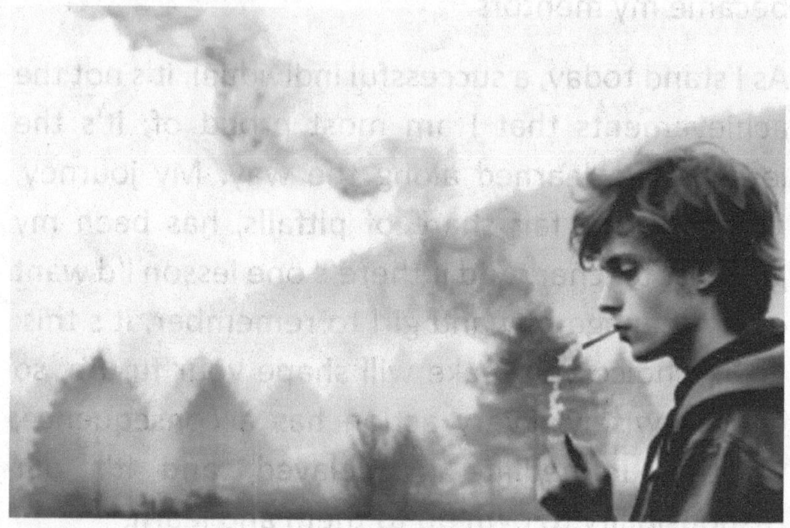

It all began at one of those house parties that defined our teenage years. Loud music, dim lights, the thrill of breaking rules, and a peculiar scent in the air that I couldn't quite place.

Jason had travelled with his family for the holiday and it was during that season I got introduced to weed. "It's just weed," Frank said, handing over a thin, hand-rolled joint. Curiosity got the better of me. After all, when you're a teenager, you're always searching for new experiences and new emotions. That night, I took my first drag.

The sensation was unlike anything I had felt before. The world around me seemed more vibrant, the music took on a different note, and my worries? They faded away, at least temporarily. And so, what began as experimentation became a habit. Frank and I would find hidden spots in Oakwood, away from prying eyes, and light up. The world felt right when I was high, but only for a short while.

However, as months turned into years, the once occasional drag became a daily ritual. I began to rely on weed to get me through the day, to cope with stress, and to escape from the reality that seemed too overwhelming.

But there were consequences, and they weren't subtle. My health began to decline; morning coughs became a routine, my once steady hands trembled often, and I found it hard to concentrate on anything for an extended period. I noticed my thoughts becoming hazier. Simple tasks felt mountainous, and my ambitions? They seemed like a distant dream.

Cooking was my passion. From a young age, the kitchen was my haven. The sound of the sizzling pan, the aroma of spices, and the joy of creating something delicious were pure magic. I dreamt of becoming a renowned chef, having my restaurant, and creating dishes that people would remember. But with my growing addiction, even cooking became challenging. I'd often burn dishes, forget ingredients, or simply lose interest midway.

My wake-up call came one fateful day in culinary school. Tasked with creating a dish that would be critiqued by renowned chefs, I found myself unable to think straight. My mind was clouded, my senses dulled. I messed up, and bad. The feedback was brutal, and for the first time, I was forced to confront the reality of what my addiction was doing to me.

Determined to get my life back on track, I sought help. Admitting you have a problem is the first step, and perhaps the most difficult one. With the support of a few close friends and rehab, I began my journey towards sobriety. The path was not easy; there were days of relapses, days when the urge was too strong. But the vision of my dream, my restaurant, kept me going.

As time passed, my health improved, and the fog that clouded my mind lifted. The world was clearer, and so were my goals. The journey of recovery taught me discipline, resilience, and the value of second chances.

Today, I stand in the heart of my restaurant, a place buzzing with energy, laughter, and the aroma of delicious food. Every dish I create is not just a blend of ingredients but a piece of my journey, my story. And while the scars of my past remain, they serve as a reminder of the lessons learned.

Chapter 5: Protect your mind

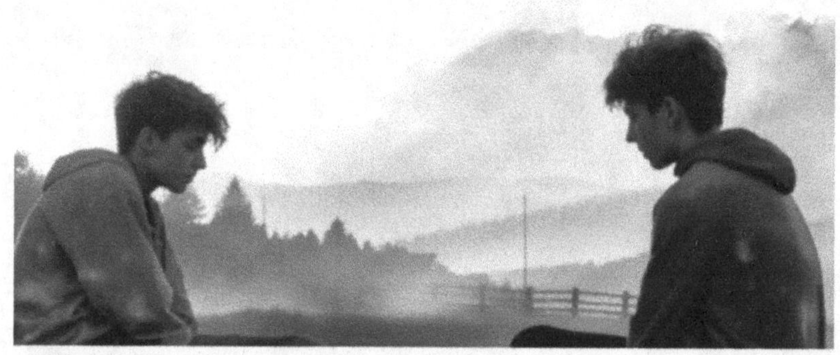

I intentionally left out some information about the days when I was addicted to weed so I could talk more in-depth about it in this chapter. Jason returned for the holiday and met a different version of me. He picked it immediately that something was off about me, but couldn't lay his finger on what it was exactly.

One day he came home unannounced and caught me smoking. But before we go on, let me tell you how badly smoking weed affected me. During the day, I would be restless, waiting for summer school to end so I could light up with my friend – Frank. Homework, which I used to excel in, became a chore. I'd often find myself staring at my textbooks, my mind wandering off to the next high. My passion for food, something that had always been my escape, started fading. Instead of experimenting with new recipes or daydreaming about running my restaurant, I was looking for the next opportunity to smoke up.

Now back to Jason's return, he had chosen a different path. He was acing his classes, was part of the school's basketball team, and had big dreams of going to college. Our paths had started to diverge, and the differences were evident.

One evening, as I was about to light up in my usual spot, Jason approached me. "You know," he began, "I miss our old times. I miss us dreaming about the future, talking about what we'd become."

I remember shrugging, "Things change."

He looked me straight in the eyes. "Yes, they do. But you're letting this control you. Remember when you cooked that three-course meal for my birthday? That's your passion. Don't lose sight of it."

His words hit hard. They began a series of questions in my mind. Was this the life I wanted?

Was the temporary high worth the permanent lows?

It took time, but I decided to confront my growing dependence on weed. It was during this time I had my culinary school exams which I failed to pass. The first step was distancing myself from those who normalized smoking weed, such as Frank. It was tough, letting go of friendships that had defined my high school life, but it was necessary.

I began diving deeper into my love for food. Cooking became my refuge. The kitchen, with its clatter and aroma, provided the same peace that the drug once promised. Only this time, it was real.

As days turned into months, and months into years, my life began to change. I finished high school with decent grades, got into a culinary school, and started my journey to become a chef. The memories of Oakwood and my tryst with weed became just that, memories.

Today, I run a successful restaurant. Every dish I create, and every praise I receive, reminds me of the choices I made, the battle I fought, and the future I carved for myself. I often think about the teenagers out there, facing the same crossroads I once stood at. If there's one thing I'd like to tell them, it's this: Protect your mind, cherish your dreams, and never let a temporary escape rob you of your permanent passion.

The road to success is paved with choices. And while it's tempting to take shortcuts, the real joy lies in the journey, in overcoming challenges, and in staying true to yourself. As for me, every time I step into my kitchen, I'm reminded of how far I've come and how much further I still have to go.

Chapter 6: Be a stoic

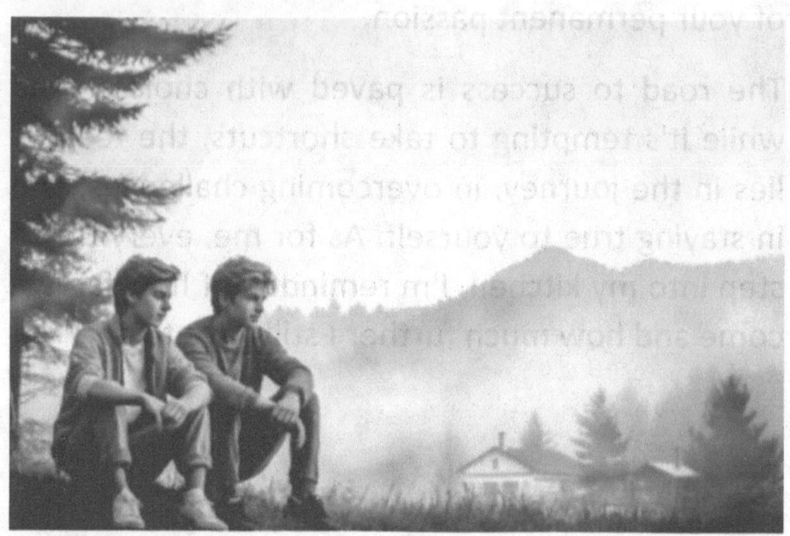

During one of my trying periods, trying to find my place in the world, I discovered the philosophy of Stoicism. It began with a book found at a garage sale. The worn-out cover and yellowed pages didn't promise much, but I was drawn to its title: "Stoicism: The Art of Embracing Calm."

The philosophy was simple, yet profound. Stoicism talks about the impermanence of life, the importance of accepting things we cannot change, and focusing on what we can control: our actions and reactions. Stoicism taught me that while we cannot control everything that happens to us, we can control our reactions. It emphasized the importance of understanding oneself, of recognizing our emotions but not being slaves to them. It became a beacon of clarity.

However, knowing the path and walking the path are two different things. The allure of my old habits was still strong. While I understood the tenets of Stoicism, practicing them was a challenge. The real test came when my best friend, Jason, fell into the trappings of drugs. Watching someone you care about tread such a dangerous path is agonizing. My initial reactions were anger and resentment. Why would he do this? Doesn't he understand the risks?

But then, the teachings of Stoicism intervened. I realized that getting angry or frustrated wouldn't help Jason. I needed to approach the situation with calm and understanding. Stoicism has taught me that people act according to their current state of mind and knowledge. Jason wasn't doing this to hurt anyone; he was lost, just like I had been.

I started engaging Jason in conversations, not confrontations. We'd sit on my porch, talking for hours about life, choices, and consequences. I shared the teachings of Stoicism with him. It's essential to recognize our emotions, and understand them, but not let them dictate our actions.

Jason, slowly but surely, began to see the light. With time and effort, he distanced himself from his previous choices, turning a new leaf. Watching his transformation reaffirmed my belief in Stoicism and its power to bring about positive change.

As the years went on, I continued to immerse myself deeper into the world of Stoicism. I joined online forums, attended seminars, and even began mentoring teenagers in the neighborhood. The journey was not without its hurdles. There were moments of doubt, moments when I thought maybe Stoicism was too passive a philosophy for the chaotic world we live in.

But every time such thoughts arose, I'd think back to my life on Oakwood Street, to the days of uncertainty and the solace Stoicism provided. I thought of Jason and the countless other lives the philosophy had touched and transformed.

Today, as I stand as a testament to the power of Stoicism, I hope to impart this wisdom to as many as I can. Especially to the young souls at the brink of life's many crossroads, unsure of which path to take. Embrace calm, understand yourself, and remember that while you can't control everything, you can control how you react. And sometimes, that makes all the difference.

Chapter 7: Love the process

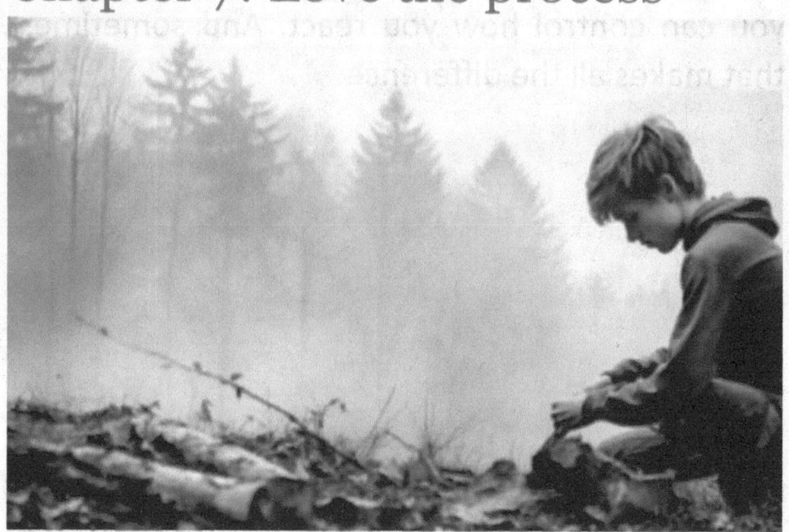

Let me take you back to a particular year that stands out. When I was less busy, not cooking or crafting menus, I would be fascinated by wood. The way I loved to crave them, one would think I would turn out to be a carpenter. There was something about taking a piece of raw wood, chiseling it, molding it, and creating something beautiful and functional. It was an art and a science.

Jason, my best mate, didn't get it at first. "Why waste time on this when you can hang with us at the park?" he'd often say. But for me, it wasn't just about the final product. It was about the process. Each piece of wood had its own story, and its own challenges, and I was determined to embrace every bit of it.

I began by creating small items like key holders and pen stands. They weren't great, not at first. But every imperfection, every failed product, taught me something new. And with every lesson, my love for the process grew. It wasn't about instant success; it was about the journey of getting there.

Of course, loving the process didn't mean it was easy. There were times when I felt like giving up. I remember one particular project; I was attempting to craft a chair. It was ambitious, something I hadn't tried before. The first time, it came out lopsided. The second, it collapsed under its weight. The third time? I accidentally drilled through my finger. That one hurt both physically and mentally.

It would've been easier to call it quits. Go back to afternoons at the park, maybe pick up a simpler hobby. But something inside me refused. It wasn't stubbornness; it was a belief in the process, a love for the journey more than the destination.

I started researching and studying different woodworking techniques. I watched countless online tutorials, practiced, made mistakes, and learned from them. Instead of shying away from challenges, I faced them head-on. Every setback, every splinter, and every hour spent in that tiny garage on Oakwood Street was a part of a much bigger picture.

By the end of that year, I had my first proper, sturdy, and, might I add, comfortable chair. Though I didn't make a living from carpentry, it taught me patience, confidence, and how to manage everyone because each wood is different. Was the chair perfect? No. But was it a result of loving and trusting the process? Absolutely.

The lessons I learned in that garage were invaluable. They taught me that real growth happens when we embrace the journey, with all its challenges and setbacks. It's about falling in love with the process, and understanding that setbacks are just setups for a bigger comeback.

Chapter 8: Start mastering a valuable skill now

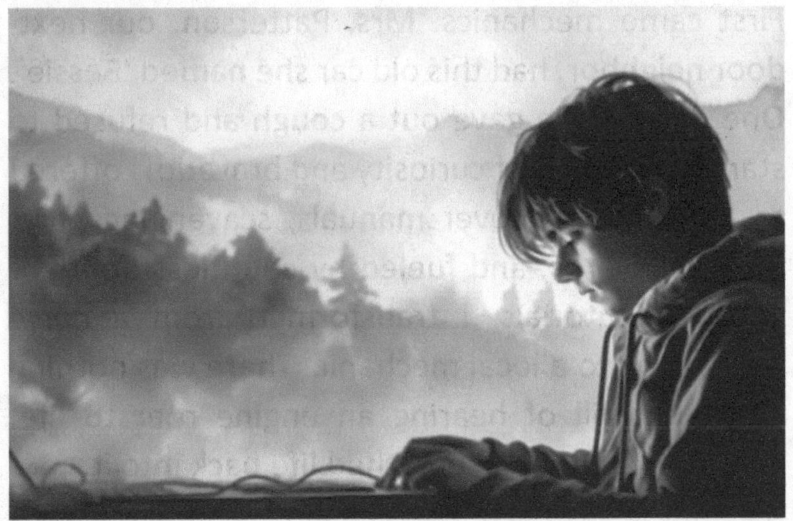

Having navigated through the siren call of drugs, I realized early that idle hands and empty hours were dangerous. With time stretching ahead and teenage restlessness taking over, I knew I had to channel my energy into something constructive.

So, one summer, the garage behind my house, which had been collecting dust and memories, became my laboratory. Inside, tools and scraps from my grandfather's carpentry days lay waiting. Carpentry had been my first love. The feel of wood, the creation of something tangible from raw materials, was magical. But as time went on, I realized there were other skills, equally tangible, waiting to be honed.

First came mechanics. Mrs. Patterson, our next-door neighbor, had this old car she named 'Bessie'. One day, Bessie gave out a cough and refused to start. With a mix of curiosity and bravado, I offered to help. Pouring over manuals, scavenging parts from junkyards, and fueled by countless hours of YouTube tutorials, I transformed from a naive teenager into a local mechanic. There was nothing like the thrill of hearing an engine roar to life, knowing your hands breathed life back into it.

However, mastering mechanics wasn't just about the skill itself; it was about the patience, perseverance, and problem-solving that came with it. It's one thing to spot an issue, but a wholly different challenge to troubleshoot and rectify it. Each setback was a lesson, each triumph, a stepping stone.

Then, my journey with music began. One evening, I stumbled upon an old guitar hidden away in the basement. Its strings were rusty, its body scratched, but it resonated with potential. While carpentry and mechanics spoke to my logical side, music touched my soul. My fingers ached, and my tunes were often off-key, but the joy of creating melodies was unparalleled.

Oakwood Street became my audience. Summer evenings were filled with strumming, singing, and the community dancing along. Music became a bridge, connecting generations and stories. Through songs, I spoke of hope, love, struggles, and dreams.

But every skill brought its challenges. There were days of utter frustration. Guitars were harder than they looked, and cars? They had minds of their own. Many times, I felt like giving up. But then I'd remember the void I was filling, the mistakes I was avoiding by being occupied. Oakwood Street had enough tales of wasted potential. I was determined not to become one.

It wasn't just about the skills, but the character they built. Every scraped knuckle, every broken guitar string, and every botched carpentry project taught me more about resilience than any book ever could. With each challenge, I learned to pick myself up, analyze my mistakes, and come back stronger.

Today, as I walk down the familiar lanes of Oakwood Street, I see young faces with dreams in their eyes. To them, I'd say: Start now. Dive into that skill you're curious about. Whether it's coding, painting, writing, or any craft, embrace it. It's not just about mastering a trade but shaping your character. Through skills, you not only create a future career but also build a shield against life's many temptations.

Oakwood, with all its stories, has been a witness to my journey. From a boy lost in its alleys to a man shaping his destiny, the skills I picked up along the way have been my guiding stars. And if a kid without a father or mentor can make it, armed with passion and perseverance, so can any teenager looking for their way.

After all, skills aren't just talents; they're tickets to a future you design.

Chapter 9: Ignore what others think of you

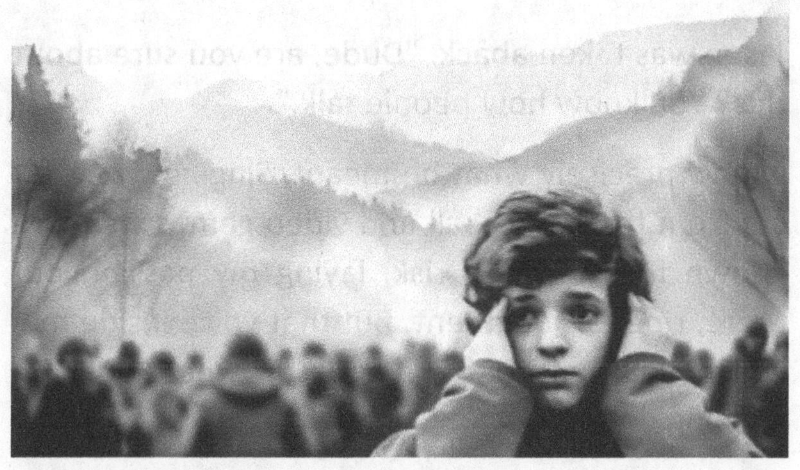

In high school, the pressure to fit in was immense. Jason and I were as thick as thieves. We shared everything: video games, basketball, and dreams of escaping Oakwood Street's narrow confines. Yet, even Jason couldn't understand the intensity with which I felt the neighborhood's eyes on me. Every stumble, every wrong move, and I'd hear it echoed in the sly comments of my classmates or the neighborhood gossip.

During our junior year, the school's annual talent show was announced. There was this burning passion inside me, a talent I had quietly honed over the years—singing. My mother said I inherited my voice from my father. She'd often tear up, hearing me hum tunes, saying how it reminded her of him. Encouraged by her, I decided to sign up for the talent show.

Jason was taken aback. "Dude, are you sure about this? You know how people talk."

I knew precisely what he meant. Singing was a far cry from the basketball and video games we were known for. It was a risk, laying my passion out there, ripe for judgment. But that voice inside me, which yearned to be heard, drowned out the echoing doubts.

Rehearsals were grueling. Every evening after school, I'd practice, refining my pitch, and controlling my breath. Days turned into weeks. The more I immersed myself in the music, the more I detached from the surrounding buzz. But it wasn't easy. The snickers, the doubtful glances, even the occasional mockery— "Look at Mr. Singer over here!"—took a toll. I'd be lying if I said I never thought about quitting. But every time I felt that way, I remembered my reason for starting in the first place: to give a voice to my passion.

The night of the talent show was a whirlwind of emotions. The auditorium was filled with familiar faces from Oakwood Street. As I waited backstage, every ounce of doubt resurfaced. The act before me, a popular dance group, left the crowd roaring. The bar was set high.

Taking a deep breath, I stepped onto the stage. The spotlight was blinding, but beyond it, I could make out the silhouettes of my audience—the entire neighborhood that had silently labeled me for years. My mind raced. But as the music started, something incredible happened. All the noise, the whispers, the judgments, faded into oblivion. All that remained was my voice, raw and real, echoing my truth.

When the song ended, for a split second, there was silence. It felt like an eternity. Then, thunderous applause broke through. The same people who had doubted, who had judged, were on their feet, clapping and cheering. But their validation, although heartwarming, wasn't my victory. My victory was over my own doubts and fears.

After that night, things changed. Not so much on Oakwood Street or at school, but within me. I realized that people would always talk, and always have opinions, but what truly mattered was how I perceived myself.

By the time senior year rolled around, I had started performing at local gigs. With every performance, my confidence grew, not just as a singer but as an individual. I learned the invaluable lesson of focusing on my own journey, undeterred by others' opinions.

Years later, Jason and I often reminisce about our Oakwood Street days. He ventured into sports journalism, while I pursued a music career, I bet you didn't know that I am a successful singer as well. But more than our achievements, it's the lessons we learned that we value most.

My journey taught me that breaking free from the shackles of others' perceptions wasn't about proving them wrong. It was about proving myself right. For every teenager walking the tumultuous path of adolescence, I'd say this: your worth is not defined by others' opinions but by the authenticity of your journey. So, drown out the noise, and let your true self echo.

Chapter 10: Be optimistic and ambitious

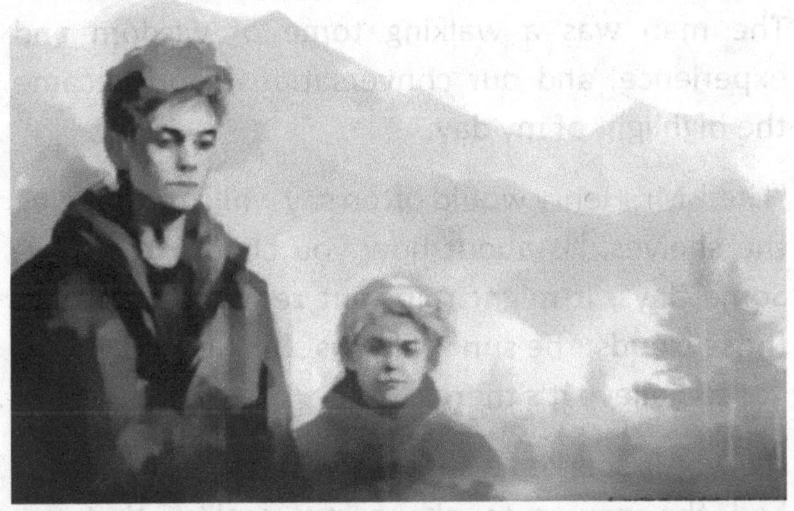

I remember those days when I would sit on the porch, my mother beside me, her face etched with wrinkles from countless worries and sleepless nights. We often struggled to make ends meet, especially after my father's departure. My teenage years were a wild mix of emotions – anger at his absence, anxiety about our financial woes, but mostly, an overwhelming confusion about my place in the world.

During those years, one could say that optimism and ambition weren't naturally in my vocabulary. But circumstances, coupled with a fiery spirit, have a funny way of steering one's path.

It all changed one summer. With school out and too much free time on my hands, I began working at Mr. Henry's convenience store down the street. The man was a walking tome of wisdom and experience, and our conversations soon became the highlight of my day.

"Life," Mr. Henry would often say while rearranging the shelves, "is about how you choose to see it. Some days, it might rain, but remember, behind those clouds, the sun is always shining. You've just got to believe it's there."

His words sparked a curiosity in me. The idea that I had the power to shape my reality, that my perspective could change my path, was intoxicating. From that moment, I made a conscious effort to view every challenge as an opportunity. This shift didn't happen overnight, but slowly, I started to notice changes.

Instead of lamenting about my father's absence, I celebrated the strength and resilience of my mother, who became my greatest role model. Rather than worrying about finances, I began to look for ways to contribute, saving up from my job and even starting small side businesses mowing lawns, or helping neighbors with chores.

One day, I sat down and penned my dreams on paper. From traveling the world to going to college and even starting my own business — the list was exhaustive. Every night, I would read them aloud, letting the sound of my ambitions resonate in the quiet of my room.

But ambition without direction is like a ship without a compass. I needed guidance. One evening, over a game of basketball, Jason said, "You know, dreaming is good, but acting on those dreams is better." He introduced me to books, courses, and mentors who had trod the path I so desired. Jason encouraged me and reminded me of my goals when I wavered and celebrated when I achieved even the smallest milestone.

But optimism and ambition come with their challenges. There were times when things didn't go as planned — when my small ventures failed or when I faced rejection. Doubt and despair often loomed large, threatening to drown my newfound enthusiasm.

It was during these low moments that I recalled Mr. Henry's words about the sun and the rain. I realized setbacks weren't stop signs; they were merely detours. Armed with this belief, I forged ahead, learning from my mistakes, and using them as stepping stones towards my dreams.

Today, I stand tall, not just as a product of Oakwood Street, but as a beacon of hope for all the kids out there who might feel trapped in their circumstances. The convenience store I once worked at? I own it now, along with a chain of others. And every summer, I hire teenagers, not just to man the cash registers, but to imbibe in them the values of optimism and ambition.

For every teen out there, remember, that your circumstances don't define you; your choices do. Dream big, stay optimistic, and let your ambitions guide you. After all, it's the challenges we face that mold us, and it's our spirit that defines the journey ahead.

Chapter 11: Success will take longer than you think

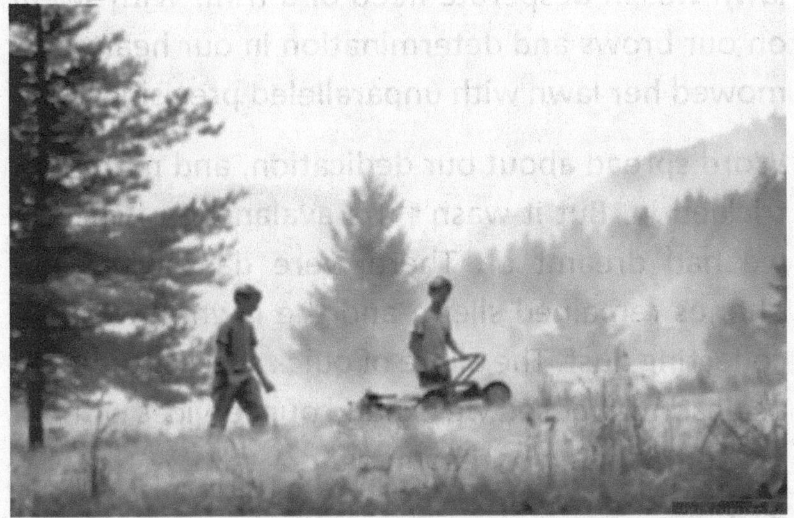

When I was 15, Jason, my best friend, and I decided to start a small business. We saw the older guys in the neighborhood mowing lawns or washing cars, and we thought, why not us? We pooled our savings and bought a couple of second-hand lawnmowers. "Green & Co.", we ambitiously named our little venture.

The start was exciting. We printed flyers, distributed them all over Oakwood, and eagerly awaited our first client. Days turned into weeks and not a single call. Doubts began to creep in. Was this a foolish idea? Did we waste our savings?

But then Mrs. Patterson, an elderly lady from down the street, gave us our first break. Her expansive lawn was in desperate need of a trim. With sweat on our brows and determination in our hearts, we mowed her lawn with unparalleled precision.

Word spread about our dedication, and more jobs trickled in. But it wasn't the avalanche of success we had dreamt of. There were days when our phones remained silent, and the lawnmowers sat collecting dust. The allure of quick success tempted us. Jason proposed we expand our services without proper planning or resources.

To keep our momentum, we borrowed money to buy equipment we didn't need. And with that, debt began to accumulate. Pressure built, and with every passing day, the weight on our young shoulders grew.

We watched as some peers seemed to easily sail to success. Like Tommy, who started a pet walking service and seemed to have struck gold. Or Jenny, who began tutoring and had a queue of kids waiting outside her door.

Comparisons are often the thief of joy, and in our case, also the thief of patience. I felt bitterness creeping in. What were we doing wrong?

One evening, a chance conversation changed my perspective. Mr. Johnson, an old-timer from Oakwood, saw me staring forlornly at our idle equipment. "You know," he started, "when I was your age, I had my share of failed businesses. It took me longer than most to find my true calling. But when I did, all those years of waiting made sense."

His words struck a chord. Was it possible that the journey to success was meant to be longer for some? That every hurdle, every delay was a lesson in disguise?

Taking this new perspective to heart, Jason and I decided to regroup. We paid off our debt, sold the unnecessary equipment, and focused solely on lawn mowing. More importantly, we learned the importance of patience. Instead of being despondent during lulls, we used that time to improve our skills, learn about customer service, and understand the value of hard work.

Over time, Green & Co. became a trusted name in Oakwood. We didn't have instant success, but when it did come, it was steady and fulfilling.

The teenage venture laid the foundation for bigger things. It instilled in me the values of persistence, patience, and the importance of not comparing my journey to others. Success, I realized, wasn't a sprint; it was a marathon.

Years later, when I ventured into larger business endeavors and faced inevitable challenges, I often revisited those Oakwood days. The lessons I learned during those formative years were invaluable.

Success might have taken longer than I anticipated, but every extra mile was worth it. Oakwood Street, Jason, and the legacy of Green & Co. weren't just memories; they were a testament to the power of perseverance and the magic that unfolds when one refuses to give up.

To the teenagers of today, eager to step into the world and make a mark: remember that your journey is unique. It might take longer, and there might be more twists and turns than you expect. But hold onto patience. In the end, it's not about how quickly you reach the destination, but the richness of the journey itself.

Chapter 12: Compare yourself to no-one

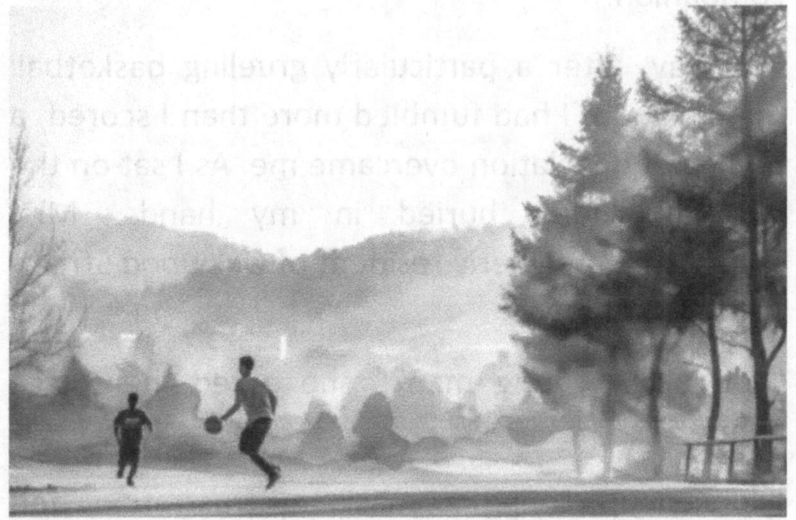

Living in a community where everyone knew everyone meant that comparisons were as common as morning greetings. Whether it was grades, sports, looks, or the brands we wore, everything seemed to be up for scrutiny. It was like living in a constant race, and every day was a struggle not to fall behind.

My friend Jason was the star basketball player in our school. With every 3-pointer he scored, his popularity soared. Then there was Rosie, the girl next door, with her flawless grades and a voice that could bring tears to anyone's eyes. Everywhere I looked, it seemed like someone was outdoing me, shining brighter, reaching higher. The pressure was immense, and self-doubt became a daily companion.

One day, after a particularly grueling basketball match where I had fumbled more than I scored, a feeling of desolation overcame me. As I sat on the curbside, head buried in my hands, Mrs. Thompson, an elderly resident of Oakwood Street, approached me.

"You okay, young man?" she asked, her voice gentle.

I looked up, trying to mask my frustration, and responded, "I just feel like no matter how hard I try, it's never good enough. Jason, Rosie... they're all doing so much better."

Mrs. Thompson sat beside me. "You know," she began, "when I was your age, Oakwood Street was a different place. We didn't have the gadgets and social media to broadcast our achievements. But the comparisons were always there. My best friend, Lily, was the town's favorite. Everything she touched turned to gold, or so it seemed. And I always felt like I was living in her shadow."

I turned to her, surprised. Mrs. Thompson was one of the most respected individuals in our community, known for her wisdom and grace. It was hard to imagine her ever feeling inferior.

Seeing my surprise, she continued, "It took me years to understand that life isn't a race against others. It's a journey where you set your milestones. Every time I compared myself to Lily, I was undermining my worth, my journey."

"But how do you stop feeling overshadowed?" I asked, my voice barely above a whisper.

"By focusing on your path," she replied. "Recognize your strengths, accept your weaknesses, and remember, every person you compare yourself to is probably fighting their battle, facing challenges you know nothing about."

Our conversation lasted for hours, and by the time we were done, the sun had set, casting Oakwood Street in a soft, golden hue.

I began to change my perspective after that day. Instead of looking at Jason's basketball skills or Rosie's achievements, I began focusing on my strengths. I had a knack for writing, and soon, I started penning down stories of Oakwood Street, capturing the essence of our community. My tales became a hit, and before I knew it, I was the editor of our school magazine.

But the journey wasn't smooth. There were moments of doubt, days when the voices in my head told me I wasn't good enough. But every time such thoughts surfaced, I remembered Mrs. Thompson's words and pushed forward.

Years later, I found myself at a reunion. The faces I once envied were all there. As we reminisced about our Oakwood days, a surprising truth emerged. Jason spoke about the immense pressure he felt as the school's star player, the fear of not living up to expectations. Rosie talked about her struggles with anxiety, and the constant need to be perfect.

That day, it became clear that comparison truly was a mirage. While it looked like others had it all, they too were battling their insecurities.

Today, as I pen down tales of life, love, and everything in between, I often think back to that summer on Oakwood Street. The lesson I learned wasn't just about not comparing myself to others, but about recognizing and valuing my journey.

Remember, your worth isn't determined by someone else's achievements. Your journey, with its ups and downs, is unique and valuable. Treasure it, for in the end, it's the lessons you learn, and the challenges you overcome, that define who you become.

Chapter 13: Keep your promises to yourself and others

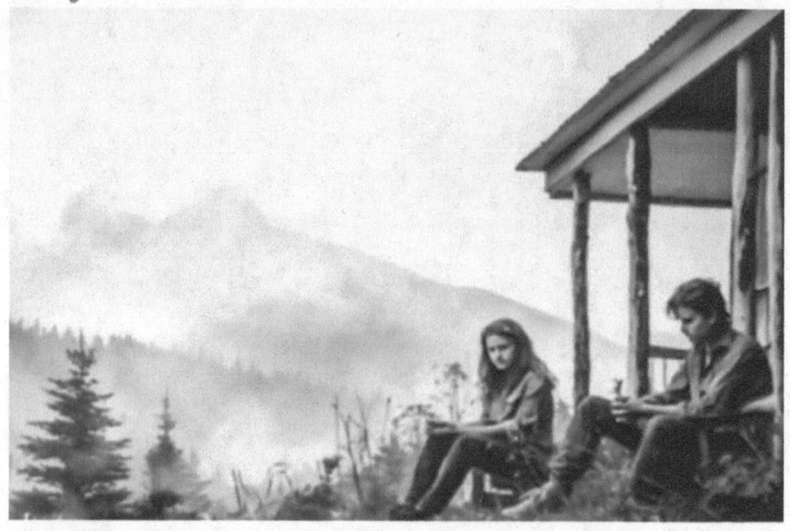

When I was 14, a small incident became a significant milestone in my life. I had promised my little sister, Maria, that I'd take her to the annual Oakwood Fair. But the same day, Jason, my best friend, got two tickets to the football match we had always dreamt of watching. The clash was evident: the long-awaited match or the promise made to Maria.

As tempting as the match was, the thought of Maria waiting excitedly for our day out was something I couldn't shake off. I kept my promise. We had an incredible day at the fair, filled with laughter, rides, and cotton candy. Later that evening, Jason told me the match wasn't that great anyway. That decision taught me a valuable lesson early on: promises made to loved ones are sacred.

But the promises I made to myself were just as vital. At 16, seeing many of my friends delve into the world of drugs and misdemeanors, I promised myself never to touch them. The temptations were everywhere. Friday nights at Oakwood saw many teens sneaking into hidden corners, lighting up their futures, quite literally, in smoke. The thrill of it, the escape it promised from the pressures of adolescence, was enticing.

One evening, as we sat at our secret spot – a quiet, serene place overlooking the city – I felt the weight of my world on my shoulders. The school was demanding, the void of not having a father figure became more profound, and the general struggles of being a teenager were taking their toll. Mike approached us, holding out a joint, "It'll make you feel better," he assured.

I remembered my promise. This wasn't about appearing 'cool' or giving in to peer pressure. It was about staying true to myself. I declined, not with a sense of superiority, but with a commitment to the path I had promised to walk on.

The teenage years are tumultuous and full of questions, doubts, and external influences. For me, the absence of a father meant searching for role models, for guidance. I often found that guidance in the promises I made.

Another such moment was when Mrs. Patterson, our elderly neighbor, needed help with her garden. I had promised to assist. But as the weekend approached, a significant basketball tournament came up. I was torn. Mrs. Patterson depended on me, but the team did too.

I approached the coach, explaining my predicament. He, understanding the gravity of my commitment, allowed me to miss the initial practice sessions. That weekend, while my team practiced, I was planting roses and mowing the lawn. Mrs. Patterson's gratitude, the joy in her eyes, was worth more than any trophy.

This approach to promises wasn't always easy. There were times I felt I was missing out. Times when I questioned if these self-set guidelines were worth the sacrifices. But as the years rolled on, the benefits became evident. People around me began to view me as reliable. I was the guy who would stick to his word, the one you could count on. That trust opened doors for me, from job opportunities to deep, meaningful relationships.

Years later, when I looked back at my life, the challenges, the crossroads, and the moments of doubt, it became clear that promises were not just words. They were commitments, not only to others but to oneself. They molded character, built trust, and laid the foundation for a life of integrity.

Remember, in those critical moments, your promises, to yourself and others, can be your guiding light. Stick to them, honor them, and you'll find your way.

Chapter 14: Learn to become self-reliant

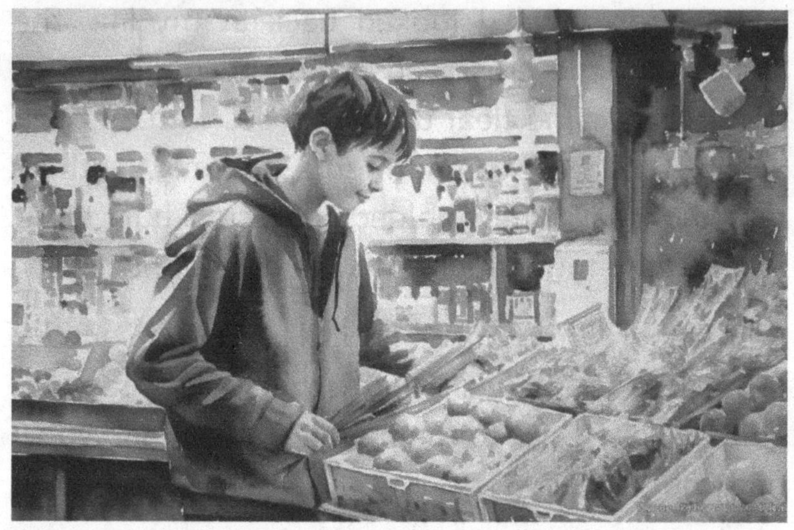

When we lost the house because we couldn't keep up with the mortgage, I had to get a job to support mum, then I took up a casual job at a local grocery store. The gig was simple; stock shelves, help customers, and collect my paycheck at the end of the week. The work was monotonous, but the income was a lifeline. With my mother working tirelessly to make ends meet, every dollar counted.

One evening, the manager, Mr. Daniels, approached me. "I've noticed your work ethic," he began, with a stern look that I couldn't quite read. "How would you like to manage the inventory?"

The role meant more responsibility and more hours, but it also meant a bump in my paycheck. Excited but nervous, I agreed. How hard could it be?

I couldn't have been more wrong. The inventory was a mess. Products were missing, documents were misfiled, and discrepancies were common. The task was Herculean, and I was in way over my head.

But admitting failure wasn't an option. So, night after night, long after the store had closed its doors, I'd sit with a mountain of paperwork, trying to make sense of the chaos. There were nights when frustration brought me to tears, and days when the weight seemed too much to bear.

One evening, as I was nearing breaking point, I remembered a piece of advice my mother once gave me, "Life will throw challenges. But remember, every challenge is just a problem looking for a solution."

With that thought, I changed my approach. Instead of feeling defeated, I broke the task down, tackling one problem at a time. I researched inventory systems and introduced checks and balances, and slowly, the mess began to clear.

The process taught me more than just inventory management. It taught me the importance of perseverance, the value of self-belief, and the power of hard work. It was my first taste of self-reliance, and it was empowering.

Things began to change. Mr. Daniels, initially skeptical, started trusting me with more responsibilities. Customers noticed the improvement, and I became the go-to person for any stock-related queries. My once-monotonous job became a source of pride.

But life, as always, had other plans.

One day, as I was heading to the store, I received a call that shook my world. My mother had been in an accident. While she was okay, the medical bills loomed large.

With my meager savings and the impending expenses, I was at a crossroads. It would've been easy to give in to despair, but the lessons from the grocery store were still fresh. Instead of panicking, I decided to act.

Using my newfound confidence, I approached Mr. Daniels with a proposal. The store had an unused space, which I suggested turning into a small café. I had noticed customers often looking for a place to sit and chat. The grocery store would benefit from increased foot traffic, and I would manage the café operations, sharing profits with the store.

To my surprise, Mr. Daniels agreed.

The café, christened "Mama's Corner" in honor of my resilient mother, was an instant hit. The steady income helped cover the medical expenses, and I had successfully turned a crisis into an opportunity. Mama's Corner didn't end there, with dedication and tenacity, it has transformed into the household name you know today.

Know this: life won't always be easy. You'll face trials that test your spirit and moments that break your heart. But remember, every challenge is an opportunity in disguise. Learn to rely on yourself, to find solutions in the chaos, and to forge your path. Because the power to shape your destiny lies within you.

Chapter 15: Prioritize your health and hygiene

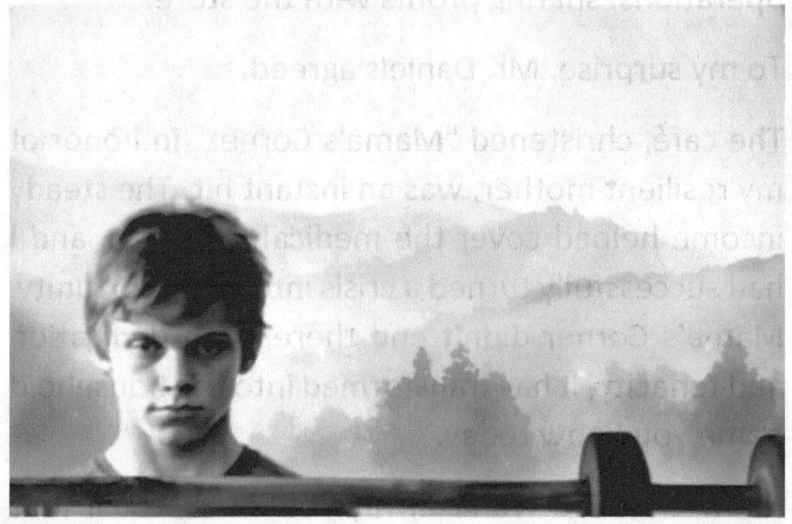

Growing up in a world of chaos, where every day was unpredictable, I often forgot the essential things in life. But if there's one thing life has taught me over the years, it's the importance of health and hygiene. This is a chapter of my journey that, in many ways, shaped the man I am today.

My early days were a whirlwind of hustling, trying to keep my head above water. I was a teenager, standing in for a father or mentor I never had, juggling responsibilities, and fighting battles. But in that fight, I neglected myself. Not having a father figure meant I missed out on some fundamental life lessons. No one told me that the food I ate, the late nights I kept, and the cleanliness I neglected would one day come back to haunt me. Although my mother tried her best, I guess boys will always be boys.

As days turned into months, my energy levels started to dip. I often found myself fatigued, unable to focus on tasks. My skin was dull, and I had constant breakouts. I assumed it was just the stress of life, but the real problem was much deeper. I was not taking care of my health and hygiene.

It all came to a head one fateful afternoon. I was playing a game of basketball with some neighborhood friends when, out of nowhere, I collapsed. The world blurred as I was rushed to the hospital.

The diagnosis was a severe vitamin deficiency coupled with exhaustion. The doctor was clear: I had to start prioritizing my health. He stressed the importance of a balanced diet, regular exercise, and maintaining personal hygiene.

At first, I was in denial. I blamed my circumstances, the lack of guidance, and the relentless pressures of life. But as I lay in that sterile hospital bed, a realization dawned on me. If I wanted a life worth living, I had to put my health first. It wasn't just about surviving; it was about thriving.

My recovery was slow but enlightening. I started with small changes. Swapping soda for water, and junk food for fruits and vegetables. I set regular sleeping hours and made it a point to wash up and keep myself clean, realizing that hygiene wasn't just about appearance; it directly impacted how I felt about myself.

I learned the hard way that our bodies are like machines. If you don't oil them regularly, they rust and break down. But if you care for them, and nourish them, they run smoothly, and efficiently, allowing you to achieve whatever you set your heart on.

Soon, I felt the difference. My energy was back. My skin cleared up, and my focus sharpened. More than the physical changes, it was the mental shift that surprised me. By taking control of my health and hygiene, I felt more in control of my life. The challenges were still there, but now I was better equipped to face them.

The journey also brought unexpected gifts. As I became more conscious of my health, I found a community of like-minded people. Together, we navigated the challenges of staying fit and healthy. I discovered the joys of cooking, the thrill of a good workout, and the satisfaction of a disciplined routine.

Looking back, that hospital visit was a wake-up call. It made me realize that health isn't just about the absence of disease; it's about holistic well-being. It's about respecting your body, giving it what it needs, and understanding that good health is the foundation of a good life.

I share this story not to preach but to highlight a lesson I learned the hard way. To every teenager reading this, remember, that your body is your most significant asset. Treat it with care, nourish it, respect it. And while life will throw many challenges your way, if you have your health, you have everything.

Because at the end of the day, health isn't just a state of the body; it's a state of mind. It gives you the strength to face life's battles, the confidence to chase your dreams, and the resilience to bounce back from setbacks.

So, as you navigate the maze of teenage life, make health and hygiene your priority. Trust me; future you will be grateful. Don't wait for a wake-up call. Start now. Your body, your future, is in your hands.

Chapter 16: Be a good student

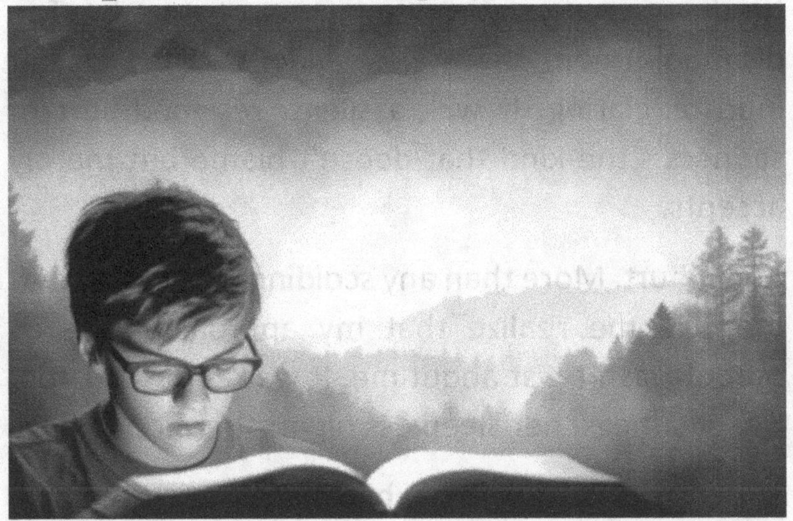

It's funny how a single moment can completely turn your life around. For me, that moment was neither an award ceremony nor a celebratory event. It was a chilly evening, sitting on the steps outside our small home, the weight of a report card heavy in my hand.

Growing up, school was never my strength. My reality was defined more by the circumstances I found myself in rather than the books I read. Homework seemed inconsequential when measured against the vast challenges of life.

Throughout middle school, I coasted. The Cs and Ds on my report card were just letters, meaningless and unrelated to my life. Until that evening.

My mother had just returned from a late shift, her tired eyes scanning my report card. The disappointment there was evident, but it wasn't loud or glaring. It was a silent, resigned sort of sadness - the kind that doesn't blame but merely accepts.

And it hurt. More than any scolding or punishment. It made me realize that my approach towards school wasn't just about me. It was about her too. Her sacrifices, her sleepless nights, her hopes.

That night, as I lay on my bed staring at the ceiling, I made a decision. I wasn't going to let my circumstances define my academic journey. I was going to rise, not just for myself, but for her too.

The next day marked the beginning of a new chapter. I reached school earlier, seeking help from teachers in subjects I struggled with. Lunchtimes were spent in the library, making up for the lessons I had ignored. Evenings, once spent wandering or hanging out with friends, were now dedicated to revision and homework.

It wasn't easy. There were days when the weight of all I had to catch up on felt unbearable. But each time I faltered, I remembered that evening and my mother's silent eyes, and it propelled me forward.

Gradually, as weeks turned into months, something shifted. Learning wasn't just about grades anymore. It was about the joy of understanding something new, the excitement of connecting the dots, and the satisfaction of solving problems. I began participating in class, asking questions, and engaging in discussions.

Soon, the Cs and Ds transformed into Bs and As. But it wasn't just about the grades. It was about the newfound respect from teachers, the admiration from peers, and the confidence that brewed within.

By the time high school ended, I had not only transformed my academic record but also my perspective on education, my extra-curricular activities like basketball and music didn't suffer as well. I realized that being a good student wasn't just about grades. It was about discipline, persistence, and a hunger for knowledge. It was about proving to myself that regardless of where I started, I controlled where I ended.

Today, the lessons from my academic turnaround stay with me. The discipline helps me in my professional life, the persistence aids me in facing challenges, and the hunger for knowledge ensures I never stop growing.

To you reading this; being a good student is not just about taking exams. It's about preparing yourself for life. It's about understanding that every class, every assignment, and every grade is a stepping stone toward becoming a better version of yourself. Don't wait for a defining moment like I did. Make every day count.

Chapter 17: Play sports or learn an instrument

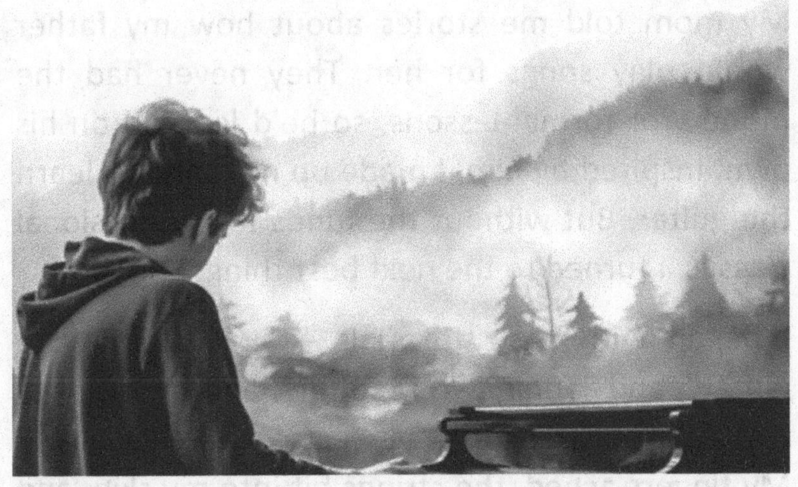

That summer, while most kids were away at camp or on vacation, I was at home, a little aimless and a lot bored. I missed the structured days of school and the constant buzz of activity. My neighborhood was quiet, with most friends away. Loneliness, a feeling I was all too familiar with.

As I was sifting through old stuff in the attic one day, trying to keep myself busy, I stumbled upon an old acoustic guitar. It had been my father's. Holding it felt like holding a part of him, a part of history. I strummed the strings, but the sound was out of tune, producing a sad, dissonant chord. But there was something about that moment – the weight of the guitar, the potential of music – that captivated me.

My mom told me stories about how my father would play songs for her. They never had the money for formal lessons, so he'd learned on his own. Inspired by him, I made up my mind to learn the guitar. But without the funds for professional classes, I turned to the next best thing: YouTube.

I began with basic tutorials – "How to hold a guitar", and "Tuning your guitar", and then slowly moved to "Basic chords". It was no walk in the park. My fingers ached, the strings bit into my skin, and there were days when I felt like giving up, thinking it was all too hard. But every time I was about to quit, I remembered the look on my mom's face when she talked about my father's playing. I wanted to give her that joy again.

Hours turned into days, days into weeks. My fingertips turned hard, calloused from the constant practice. My initial, awkward attempts at playing 'Twinkle Twinkle Little Star' evolved into more complex tunes. Each video lesson was a step forward. I would pause, rewind, and play again, ensuring I got each note right.

One day, while exploring deeper into YouTube's vast musical universe, I stumbled upon a video titled "The Power of Music". It was a TED talk by a renowned musician about the therapeutic and developmental benefits of learning an instrument. He spoke about how playing an instrument engages every part of the brain, improving cognitive functions, enhancing memory, and teaching discipline. It was a revelation. Here I was, thinking I was just fighting off boredom when in reality, I was nurturing my brain and soul.

Months passed, and the first strums of summer turned into melodies of autumn. One evening, as the sun cast a golden hue on our living room and I was engrossed in perfecting a particularly challenging piece, I didn't notice my mom had walked in. As the last note resonated in the room, she began clapping, tears streaming down her face. "That was your father's favorite song," she whispered.

That moment was worth all the hours of practice, and all the moments of frustration. The guitar, and the discipline it instilled in me, became a bridge. A bridge to my father's memory, to my mother's heart, and a stronger version of myself.

YouTube, often dismissed as just another entertainment platform, was my teacher. It showed me that learning isn't confined to classrooms. It taught me patience, perseverance, and the joy of self-accomplishment.

The world is full of resources, waiting for you to tap into them. Be it sports, an instrument, or any skill you want to acquire — if you have the passion, the world has the means. Embrace the journey, cherish the lessons, and always remember — every challenge and every hurdle is a note in the beautiful song of life.

Chapter 18: Choose your friends wisely

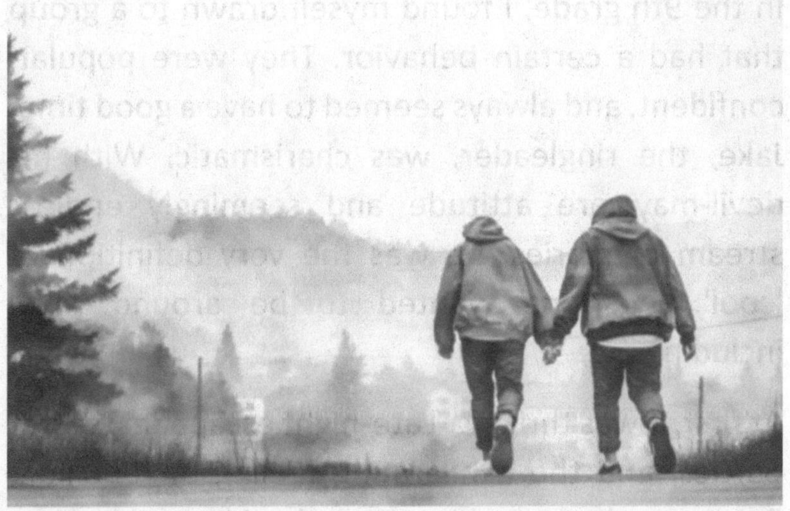

Life, as I've learned, is a series of choices. But it's not just the big ones—where to study, whom to marry, or which career to follow—that shape us. Sometimes, it's the seemingly insignificant decisions that have the most profound impact. Choosing my friends was one such decision. Specifically, the choice I made when I met Jason.

Growing up, I was a bit of a misfit. My mother worked tirelessly working to make ends meet, I often found myself turning to my peers for validation. A dangerous game for a teenager, especially when the company you keep might not always have your best interests at heart.

In the 9th grade, I found myself drawn to a group that had a certain behavior. They were popular, confident, and always seemed to have a good time. Jake, the ringleader, was charismatic. With his devil-may-care attitude and seemingly endless stream of stories, he was the very definition of 'cool'. Everyone wanted to be around Jake, including me.

At first, it was thrilling. Late-night escapades, secret parties, and the exhilarating feeling of rebellion. But as weeks turned into months, I began to see a pattern. Jake and his crew didn't have boundaries. They'd skip school, disrespect teachers, and most worrying of all, had a penchant for shoplifting.

One evening, things took a turn. Jake had devised a plan to break into the school's storeroom. "Think about it, all those expensive gadgets just waiting for us," he'd said with a glint in his eye. I remember the weight of that decision. On one hand, was the promise of more popularity and acceptance. On the other, a voice, faint but persistent, reminded me of who I was, of the principles my mother had instilled in me.

That night, I made an excuse and didn't join Jake and his group. The next morning, whispers filled the school corridors. Jake and his crew had been caught, red-handed. Watching them being led away by the school's security and the sheer disappointment on our principal's face was a wake-up call.

Amidst this chaos, I noticed Jason. A boy from my class, always in the background, never indulging in the reckless bravado of teenage life. He approached me, "You dodged a bullet last night."

We began to talk, initially about the incident, but gradually our conversations grew deeper. We spoke about our dreams, our fears, and our aspirations. Jason came from a stable family but had his battles. He'd lost a sibling in a car accident and had turned to books as his refuge.

Jason introduced me to a world I'd never known. A world of ideas, art, and music. Saturdays were no longer about recovering from a hangover but were filled with visits to the library, exploring new bands, and painting. I realized I had found a friend who didn't just want to hang out but was invested in my growth, as I was in his.

Months turned into years. College came and went. Jason and I went to different cities and pursued different careers, but our bond remained strong. Our choices led us on paths that were both fulfilling and aligned with our values.

Today, when I look back, I realize the importance of that one choice I made in 9th grade. It wasn't just about avoiding trouble; it was about defining who I was. Friends, as I've learned, are the family we choose. They influence our choices, shape our perspectives, and play a pivotal role in who we become.

Jake? Well, after a series of run-ins with the law, he eventually turned his life around. We're not in touch, but I genuinely hope he's found his path.

As for Jason and me, our friendship is a testament to the fact that true connections are built on mutual respect, shared values, and a genuine concern for each other's well-being.

Remember, the company you keep will define you. It's easy to be swayed by the allure of popularity or the thrill of rebellion. But true friendships? They stand the test of time, challenge you, uplift you, and most importantly, help you become the best version of yourself. Choose wisely.

Chapter 19: Show gratitude to your parents

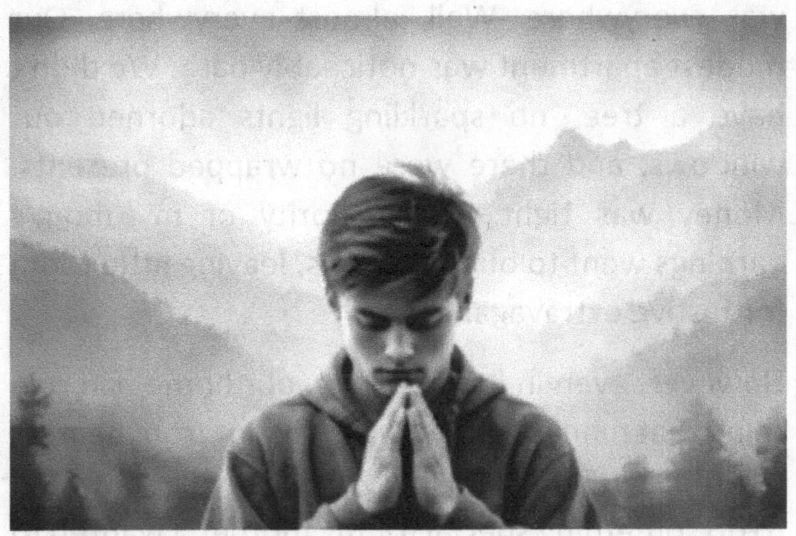

Growing up, It wasn't always easy to articulate what I felt, especially when it came to my profound gratitude towards my mother. As I grew older, I realized that saying "thank you" was just one way of expressing gratitude. True appreciation came from my actions and understanding of her sacrifices.

One winter, the memory of which still warms my heart, was the turning point in my relationship with my mother. It was the winter of my 16th year, a period where teenage angst was at its peak and where I often felt misunderstood. But, amidst all the chaos of adolescence, a revelation occurred to me: maybe I was the one not trying to understand.

Christmas was approaching, and the holiday spirit was everywhere. Well, almost everywhere. Our modest apartment was noticeably bare. We didn't have a tree, no sparkling lights adorned our windows, and there were no wrapped presents. Money was tight. The majority of my mom's earnings went to our essentials, leaving little room for festive extravagances.

However, even in its simplicity, our home had one thing that many lacked – warmth, not from heaters or fireplaces, but from love. But that year, I wanted to do something special for my mother. I wanted to show her how much her sacrifices, her hard work, and her love meant to me.

I took up odd jobs after school, saving up bit by bit. From shoveling snow for the neighbors to babysitting, I did whatever I could. Every evening, I'd come home, tired and cold, but the idea of bringing a smile to my mom's face kept me going.

With the money I gathered, I decided to recreate one of her cherished memories. When I was younger, she'd often talk about her childhood Christmases. The centerpiece of those stories was always the traditional family dinner, with roast turkey, cranberry sauce, and her favorite — a homemade pumpkin pie.

I secretly reached out to her best friend, Aunt Marie, who was more than happy to help. She handed me a recipe card written in my grandmother's elegant handwriting — the famous pumpkin pie.

The days leading up to Christmas were a blur of preparations. I'd come home from my part-time work, and when mom was asleep, practiced my cooking skills. There were a few burnt pies and overcooked turkeys, but with each attempt, I got better.

Christmas Eve arrived. With Aunt Marie's help, I managed to send my mom for a day out — a spa treat funded by her friend as her Christmas gift. In her absence, our apartment transformed. A small Christmas tree, twinkling lights, and the aroma of a sumptuous dinner filled the air.

When she walked in, the look on her face was unforgettable. Tears glistened in her eyes as she took in the scene — the recreation of her cherished memory. We sat down for dinner, and with each bite, I could see her traveling down memory lane, reliving those golden days.

But the highlight of the evening was when I handed her a small wrapped box. Inside was a pendant – a simple silver heart. "This is to remind you," I whispered, "that even if I don't say it often, I carry your love in my heart, always grateful for everything."

That night, words were unnecessary. The dinner, the pendant, the effort – they spoke volumes more than a mere "thank you" ever could.

Winter stands as a testament to the importance of showing gratitude. It's not about grand gestures, but understanding, acknowledging, and appreciating the silent sacrifices our loved ones make.

Gratitude isn't just a word. It's an action, a feeling, a realization. It bridges gaps, heals wounds, and strengthens bonds. Showing appreciation, especially to our parents, reminds us of our roots, our values, and the love that shapes us. It's not about repaying them but acknowledging that their love is the foundation on which we build our futures.

...

Things didn't end there... The years that followed that special winter were a whirlwind of growth and transformation. My relationship with my mother deepened and matured. The walls of teenage resentment and anger slowly crumbled, replaced with understanding and appreciation. But as one wound healed, another, older and deeper one, begged for attention: the gnawing pain of an absent father.

As a teenager, I'd often brushed aside thoughts of my father. I was convinced he had abandoned us and left us to face the world's challenges alone. The narrative I'd constructed in my mind was one of betrayal, and for years, it felt easier to hold onto the resentment than face the pain.

However, life has a way of bringing old wounds to the surface. One crisp spring day, a letter arrived. The handwriting was unfamiliar, yet something deep within me sensed its origin. Tearing it open, I found a note from a man identifying himself as a friend of my father's.

The letter spoke of my father's recent diagnosis of terminal cancer and his desire to reconnect. He'd been asking about me and had expressed regret about the years lost. The man wrote of my father's profound remorse for the choices he made and his hope to make amends before it was too late.

The emotions that surged were overwhelming. Anger, pain, confusion, and surprisingly, a faint glimmer of curiosity. Memories of my father, previously buried deep, started to resurface. But instead of the negative ones, I remembered the moments before he left - his laughter, the stories he told, the way his eyes lit up when he saw me.

I decided to reply.

That letter turned into a meeting, and soon, I found myself face to face with the man I once called "Dad". He was frail, a shadow of the strong man from my memories. But in his eyes, I saw the same warmth, clouded by years of pain and regret.

Over coffee, he spoke about his life after leaving us. It wasn't filled with adventures or newfound freedom as I'd imagined. Instead, it was a tale of struggles, loneliness, and profound guilt. His reasons for leaving were complex, rooted in his insecurities, mental health issues, and external pressures. As I listened, I realized that while his actions hurt us deeply, he, too, was a victim of his demons.

We began meeting frequently, and with each visit, layers of resentment peeled away. I introduced him to parts of my life, sharing my achievements, failures, and dreams. And he, in turn, opened up about his life, filling the gaps of the years we were apart.

One day, during a particularly emotional conversation, he expressed his deepest regret – not being there when I needed him. Tears streaming down his face, he whispered, "I'm so sorry." It was a simple sentence, yet it carried the weight of decades of pain.

And in that moment, forgiveness felt natural. Not just for him but for myself, for holding onto the anger for so long.

Our reconciliation journey wasn't just about words. I took him to chemotherapy sessions, holding his hand through the tough days, and celebrating the small victories. We visited places from our past, reminiscing about the good times and addressing the painful ones.

One day, near the end, I presented him with a framed photo of us from my childhood, capturing a moment of pure joy. It was my way of showing gratitude, acknowledging our past, and cherishing the time we had now. He kept that picture by his bedside till the end, a testament to our rekindled bond.

His passing was a painful chapter, but the grief was tinged with gratitude. I was thankful for the opportunity to mend our relationship, to understand him, and more importantly, to forgive.

The journey with my father taught me that life is too short for resentment. Forgiveness doesn't mean forgetting; it means choosing to remember without pain. It means understanding that everyone, including our parents, is human, with flaws and battles. And sometimes, showing gratitude is about giving them, and ourselves, a second chance.

Chapter 20: Focus on the present

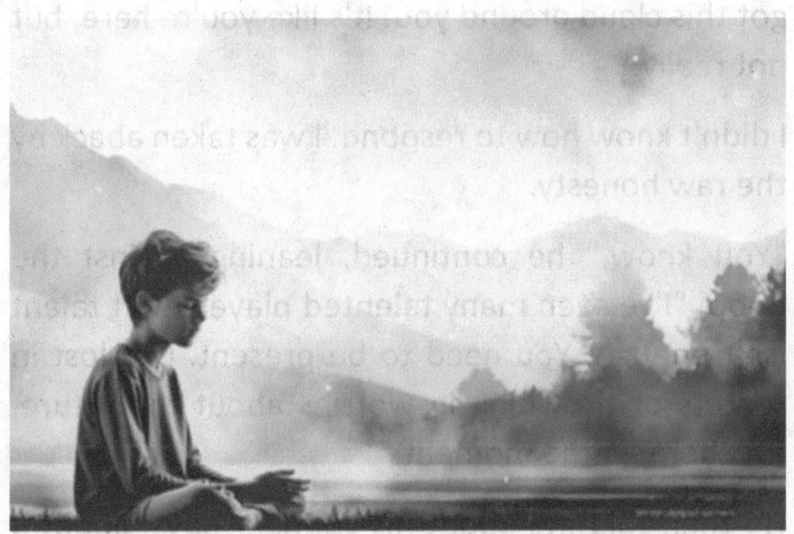

During my high school years, I became part of the school's basketball team. It was the one place where I felt like I belonged, where my worries momentarily paused. On that court, there was no yesterday or tomorrow, just the game. But off the court, the weight of the world returned, heavier than before.

One evening, after a particularly grueling practice session, our coach, Mr. Roberts, asked me to stay back. I remember the conversation vividly, not for the words he used but for the impact they had on my life.

"You're one of the best players I've seen," he began, wiping the sweat off his brow, "but you've got this cloud around you. It's like you're here, but not really."

I didn't know how to respond. I was taken aback by the raw honesty.

"You know," he continued, leaning against the hoop, "I've seen many talented players, but talent isn't enough. You need to be present. Not lost in regrets or drowning in worries about the future. Just here, in the moment."

He then told me about his younger days, about a major accident that almost claimed his life. Post the accident, he had been consumed with anger and regret, constantly asking 'why me?'. Then one day, as he watched the sunset, it hit him. While he had been agonizing over a past he couldn't change and a future he couldn't predict, life was passing him by.

"That sunset taught me to live in the present. To cherish every moment. Not to be bound by what was or paralyzed by what might be. That's the secret, son. Focus on the now."

His words resonated with me. I realized that by being trapped in the past and the future, I was missing out on the beauty of the present. It was as if I was watching a movie, constantly rewinding or fast-forwarding, never really enjoying the story.

I started small, dedicating a few minutes each day to just sit and observe - the rustling of the leaves, the distant sounds of the city, or just the rhythm of my breathing. It wasn't easy. My mind frequently wandered back to its usual patterns. But with time and persistence, I felt a change.

School assignments that previously felt daunting were now tackled with better concentration. Relationships improved as I genuinely listened and engaged in conversations. And most importantly, the gaping void I felt due to the absence of my father began to heal. Not because the situation changed, but because I started to accept the present for what it was.

During a backpacking trip across the state, the lesson of staying present was driven home. While trekking up a particularly challenging trail, I caught myself worrying about the journey ahead. The weight of my backpack, the uncertainty of the path, and the setting sun, all fed my anxieties. But then, I remembered Mr. Robert's words.

I paused, taking a deep breath. Instead of worrying about the path ahead, I began focusing on each step. I felt the ground beneath my boots, listened to the wind, and observed the shades of the setting sun. The shift was transformative. Not only did the journey become more manageable, but I also started enjoying it.

Whether it was studying, playing, or simply conversing with someone, I made a conscious effort to be 'there'. And the more I practiced it, the clearer things became. My game improved, my relationships deepened, and most importantly, I found peace.

It wasn't easy. Old habits die hard, and there were times I'd slip back into the chasm of what-ifs and if-only. But with time and persistence, the present became my home.

Today, years later, I'm armed with the wisdom that the present is all we truly have. It's the canvas on which we paint our stories, filled with colors of joy, strokes of challenges, and shades of experiences.

I want you to know that life is a series of moments. Don't let the shadows of the past or the uncertainty of the future steal the light of your present. Embrace it, live it, cherish it. Because the present is where life happens. It's where dreams are born, battles are fought, and memories are made. Don't miss out on your story by focusing elsewhere. The present moment is a gift, unwrap it with all your heart.

Chapter 21: Enjoy being a kid

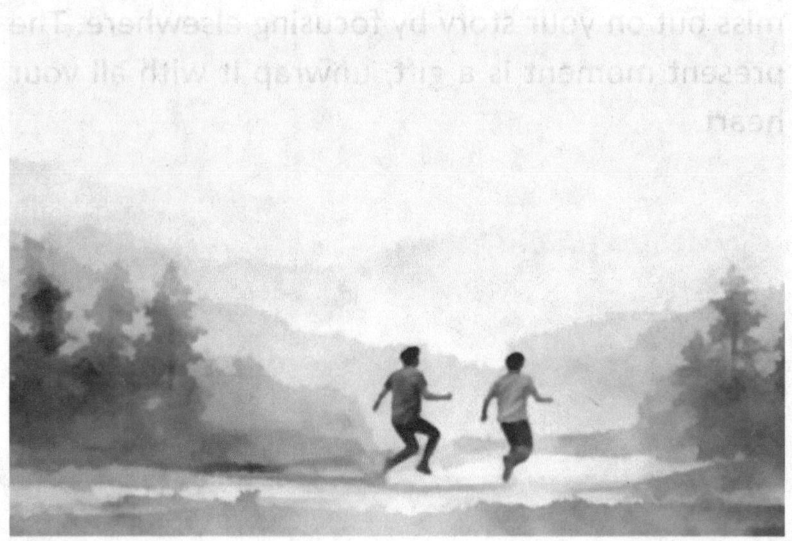

Having a single parent isn't something I'd wish on anyone. But in retrospect, those early years shaped me, teaching me things that I'd never learn from textbooks. One of the most enduring lessons from that time? The importance of truly enjoying childhood. Here's why.

The world seemed bigger when I was a kid. Every nook and cranny of my neighborhood was an uncharted territory, every tree a potential treehouse, every puddle an ocean waiting to be crossed. The limitations of adulthood hadn't clouded my horizon; there was no mortgage to worry about, no bills to pay, and no obligations other than the simple ones — like being home before the streetlights came on.

But not having a father around often made me feel like I had to grow up faster than the other kids. The absence of that paternal guidance weighed heavily on me. There were moments when I felt I had to be 'the man of the house,' even though my shoes were still filled with growing feet.

One particular summer stands out. I was around 10, and like many kids my age, I had a bike. It wasn't anything fancy, but it was mine. On this bike, I was free. I remember the wind on my face, the feeling of speeding downhill, the crunch of gravel under the tires, and the pure, unadulterated joy of being alive and in the moment.

One day, on a whim, I decided to go on an 'adventure.' I packed a small backpack with a sandwich, an apple, and a bottle of water. With a paper map drawn by my imaginative hand, marking 'treasures' and 'dragon lairs,' I set off. The journey took me through streets I'd never been down before, past houses with kids playing in yards, laughing and shouting. I felt like a true explorer, discovering new worlds.

Somewhere along the way, I met Emma. She was about my age, with fiery red hair and a spirit to match. Seeing my map, she asked if she could join my adventure. That day, we fought imaginary dragons, found 'hidden treasures,' and even saved a 'princess' (a friendly neighborhood cat). As the sun began to set, we sat on a hill, looking over our 'kingdom,' sharing stories of our exploits and dreams for the future.

What I remember most about that day isn't the adventures we crafted but the simplicity of it all. The freedom to be a kid, to imagine, to explore, and to connect with another human being without the constraints and preconceptions of adulthood.

As I grew older, the pressures of life began to pile up. School, work, relationships, responsibilities — they all started demanding my attention. The simplicity of that summer day with Emma seemed like a distant memory. But every time life got overwhelming, I'd close my eyes and transport myself back to that hill, feeling the soft grass under my palms and the warmth of the setting sun on my face.

Why is it essential to cherish childhood, you ask? Because it's the only time in your life when you are allowed — no, expected — to dream without boundaries. It's a time when the world is your playground, where every challenge is an adventure waiting to be tackled, where friendships are pure, and where the future is a bright canvas waiting to be painted.

Today, as I walk through the complexities of adulthood, the lessons from that summer day guide me. They remind me to approach life with the wonder of a child, to cherish the simple moments, and to always keep that spark of imagination alive. Because if you can hold onto the essence of your childhood — the curiosity, the joy, the resilience — you'll find that the world remains a place of endless possibilities.

To every teenage boy or girl reading this: Take it from someone who had to grow up too soon. Don't rush your youth. Relish every moment, every giggle, every dream. Climb trees, chase fireflies, invent worlds, and always, always believe in the magic of now. Because one day, when life's burdens weigh you down, these memories will be your sanctuary, a testament to the time when you truly understood what it meant to be alive.

Conclusion

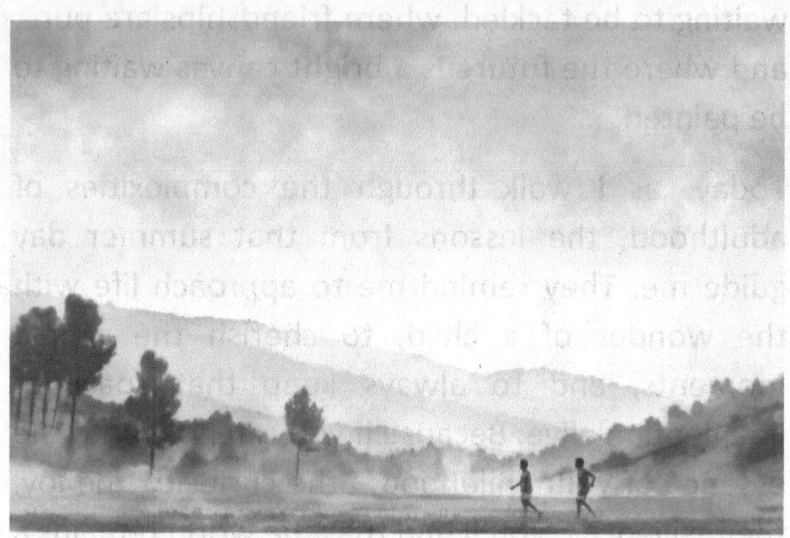

had a lot of questions growing up. Without a father to guide me, and with life throwing challenges at every turn, it often felt like I was on a ship in a stormy sea, without a compass. Sometimes, the winds were so strong I thought I'd be thrown overboard. But here I am today, still standing, stronger and wiser.

Why? Because throughout my journey, I learned. I watched, listened, fell down, got up, and made choices. Some are good, some not so good. But every single experience taught me something. And I believe that these lessons, 21 of them to be exact, can help you too.

Remember the time I talked about enjoying being a kid? It seems simple, right? But it's more profound than it appears. As a kid, your primary job is to learn and explore. So, when you rush to grow up, you miss out on this critical phase. Trust me, adulthood comes with its own set of challenges, and you'll have enough time for that. Enjoy the playground while you can. Feel the wind in your hair as you swing high. Laugh out loud with your friends. Make memories. They will be your anchor in the tough times.

Then there's the lesson about being self-reliant. Life isn't always fair. Sometimes, you'll find yourself alone, without anyone to lean on. That's when being self-reliant becomes vital. It's not just about doing things for yourself but knowing that you can face challenges and find solutions. It's the confidence that whatever life throws at you, you'll figure it out.

I also touched upon some harder topics, like the importance of staying away from substances. It's a tricky one, especially when you see others around you trying it out. But I've been down that road, and I promise you, it's not worth it. The momentary high is not worth the long-term consequences.

Your body and mind are your most valuable assets. Take care of them.

Now, let's talk about friends. Jason, my best friend, was a pillar of support for me. He and I shared many memories and learned a lot together. Friends are the family you choose. Surround yourself with people who lift you up, who challenge you, who laugh with you, and who are there during the hard times.

Looking back, I realize that every challenge, every setback, was a lesson in disguise. It was preparing me for bigger things, shaping me into the person I am today. And as you step into the world, ready to make your mark, remember that life is full of lessons. Every experience, good or bad, has something to teach.

In this book, I've tried to share the essence of my journey. Not to say that my way is the only way, but to offer a helping hand, a beacon of light. I hope these stories and lessons resonate with you, give you hope during the tough times, and remind you to celebrate the good ones.

Teenagers, as you move forward, remember that life is an incredible journey. There will be highs and lows, sunny days, and stormy nights. But with each step, you'll grow. Learn from every experience, cherish every moment, and remember that you're not alone. We've all been there, and we're cheering for you. Embrace the journey, take the lessons to heart, and most importantly, believe in yourself.

To a future filled with adventures, lessons, and countless memories. Cheers!

If You Enjoyed This Book, Please Don't Hesitate to Leave Us a Review on amazon. Thanks

Follow The Author Ali Welch

If you have any Inquiries Write to us at

Murdlepooper@gmail.com